Great Songs by
THE LADIES

784.61 GRE

Project Manager: Zobeida Pérez
Art Design & Layout: Lisa Greene Mane

CONTENTS

All I Wanna Do – **Sheryl Crow** 16

Anything for You – **Gloria Estefan** 9

Bag Lady – **Erykah Badu** 154

Beautiful Stranger – **Madonna** 85

Blue Bayou – **Linda Ronstadt** 29

Can't Fight the Moonlight – **LeAnn Rimes** 80

Constant Craving – **k. d. lang** 76

Don't Let Go (Love) – **En Vogue** 96

Ex-Girlfriend – **No Doubt** 183

Feel Like Makin' Love – **Roberta Flack** 14

For You I Will – **Monica** 109

For Your Eyes Only – **Sheena Easton** 41

Get Here – **Oleta Adams** 48

Hopelessly Devoted to You – **Olivia Newton-John** 66

How Do I Live – **Trisha Yearwood** 114

I Love You Always Forever – **Donna Lewis** 101

I Say a Little Prayer – **Diana King** 192

I Still Believe – **Mariah Carey** 70

I Turn to You – **Christina Aguilera** 198

I Want You to Need Me – **Celine Dion** 139

I Will Love Again – **Lara Fabian** 204

I Will Remember You – **Sarah McLachlan** 218

I Will Survive – **Gloria Gaynor** 209

Inseparable – **Natalie Cole** 214

It's My Turn – **Diana Ross** 24

Just Because – **Anita Baker** *34*

MacArthur Park – **Donna Summer** *222*

Need to Be Next to You – **Leigh Nash of Sixpence None the Richer** *232*

New Attitude – **Patti LaBelle** *144*

Nobody Does It Better – **Carly Simon** *106*

One Moment in Time – **Whitney Houston** *4*

Oops!...I Did It Again – **Britney Spears** *132*

Out Here on My Own – **Irene Cara** *118*

Over the Rainbow – **Judy Garland** *236*

People – **Barbra Streisand** *121*

Piano in the Dark – **Brenda Russell** *124*

Remember Me This Way – **Jordan Hill** *240*

The Rose – **Bette Midler** *44*

Save the Best for Last – **Vanessa Williams** *246*

Still – **Alanis Morissette** *169*

Strong Enough – **Cher** *53*

Sunny Came Home – **Shawn Colvin** *254*

That's the Way – **Jo Dee Messina** *92*

Theme From Ice Castles (Through the Eyes of Love) – **Melissa Manchester** *251*

This Kiss – **Faith Hill** *260*

Together Again – **Janet Jackson** *176*

Try Again – **Aaliyah** *149*

Un-Break My Heart – **Toni Braxton** *164*

The Way I Want to Touch You – **Captain & Tenille** *129*

What's Love Got to Do With It – **Tina Turner** *60*

You Needed Me – **Anne Murray** *264*

You Were Meant for Me – **Jewel** *268*

You're Still the One – **Shania Twain** *161*

ONE MOMENT IN TIME

Words and Music by
ALBERT HAMMOND and JOHN BETTIS

Each day I live, I want to be a day to give the best of me. I'm on-ly one, but not a-lone. My fin-est day is yet un-

6

ANYTHING FOR YOU

Words and Music by
GLORIA ESTEFAN

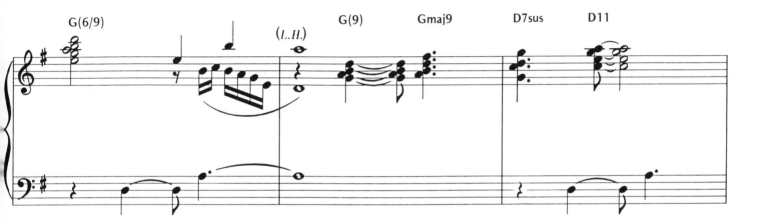

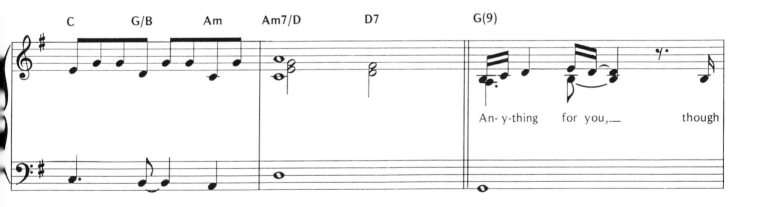

Anything for You - 5 - 1

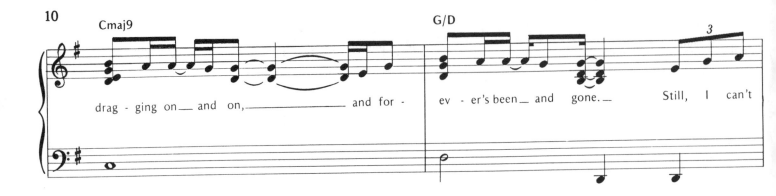

drag - ging on — and on, _____ and for - ev - er's been — and gone. __ Still, I can't

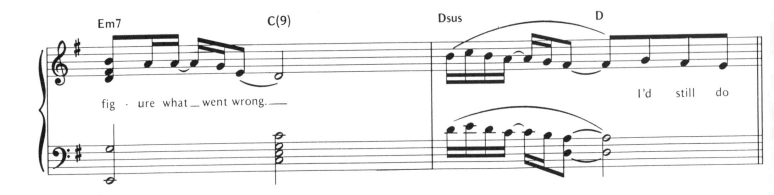

fig - ure what — went wrong. __ I'd still do

an - y-thing for you; — I'll play your game. __ You hurt me through and through, but you can

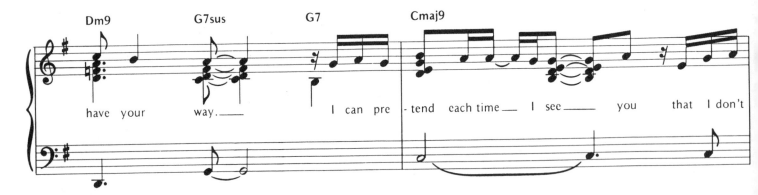

have your way. __ I can pre -tend each time — I see ___ you that I don't

care and I don't need ___ you. And though you'll nev - er see — me cry - ing; you know, in-

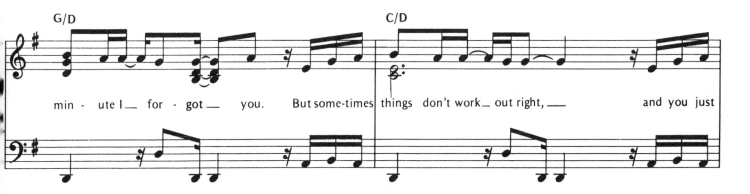

Anything for You - 5 - 3

care, and nev-er leave ____ you. But if that some-one ev - er hurts ____ you, you just might

dim.

need a friend ___ to turn to. And I'd do

p

an - y-thing for you; ___ I'll give you up, ____ if

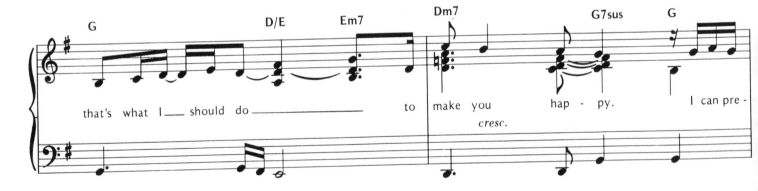

that's what I ___ should do _____ to make you hap - py. I can pre -

cresc.

tend each time ___ I see ___ you that I don't care and I don't need ___ you. And though in-

mf

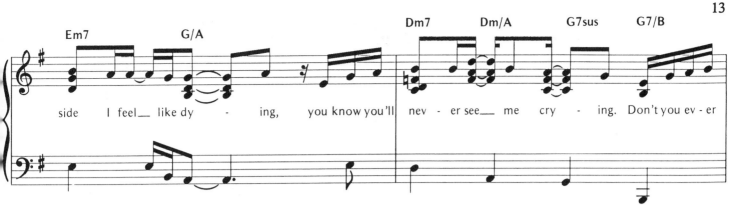

side I feel__ like dy - ing, you know you'll nev - er see__ me cry - ing. Don't you ev - er

think that I don't love____ you, that for one min - ute I for-got____ you. But some-times

things don't work our right,_____ and you just have to say__ good - bye._____

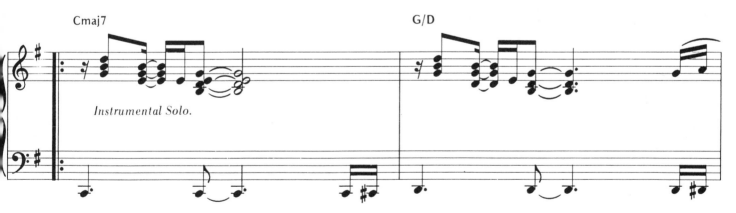

Instrumental Solo.

Repeat ad lib. and fade

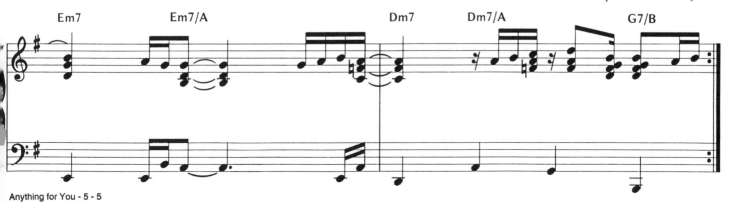

Anything for You - 5 - 5

FEEL LIKE MAKIN' LOVE

Words and Music by
EUGENE McDANIELS

ALL I WANNA DO

Words and Music by
SHERYL CROW, WYN COOPER, KEVIN GILBERT,
BILL BOTTRELL and DAVID BAERWALD

All I Wanna Do - 8 - 1

18

un - til the sun comes up o - ver San - ta Mon - i - ca Boul - e - vard.

Verse 3:
I like a good beer buzz early in the morning,
And Billy likes to peel the labels from his bottles of Bud
And shred them on the bar.
Then he lights every match in an oversized pack,
Letting each one burn down to his thick fingers
Before blowing and cursing them out.
And he's watching the Buds as they spin on the floor.
A happy couple enters the bar dancing dangerously close to one another.
The bartender looks up from his want ads.
(To Chorus:)

IT'S MY TURN

Words by
CAROLE BAYER SAGER

Music by
MICHAEL MASSER

And if liv-ing for my-self is what I'm guilt-y of, go on and sen - tence me, I'll still be free.

It's my turn to see what I can see, I hope you'll un-der-stand,

It's My Turn - 5 - 1

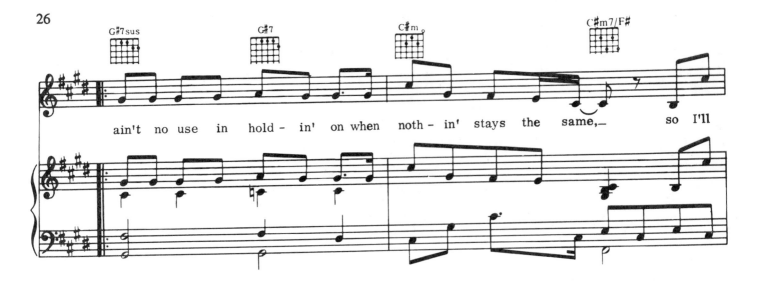

ain't no use in hold-in' on when noth-in' stays the same,— so I'll

let it rain, 'cause the rain ain't gon-na hurt___ me, and I'll

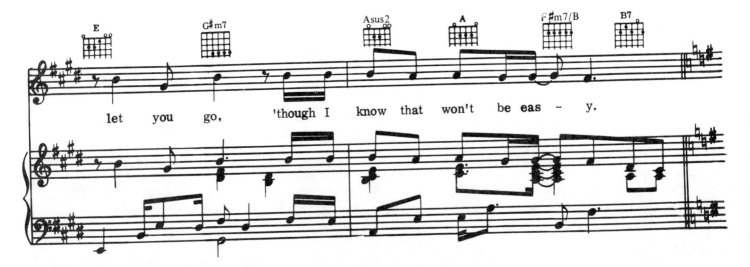

let you go, 'though I know that won't be eas-y.

It's My Turn - 5 - 5

BLUE BAYOU

Words and Music by
ROY ORBISON and JOE MELSON

where the folks are fine__ and the world is mine on Blue Bay-ou;__

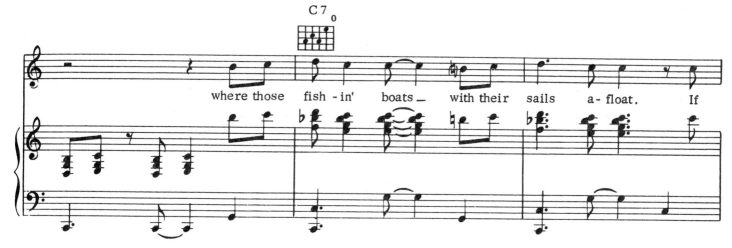

where those fish-in' boats__ with their sails a-float. If

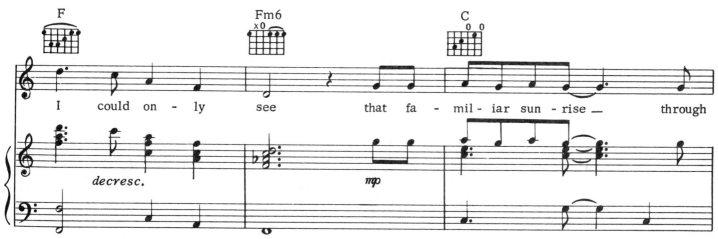

I could on-ly see that fa-mil-iar sun-rise__ through

decresc. *mp*

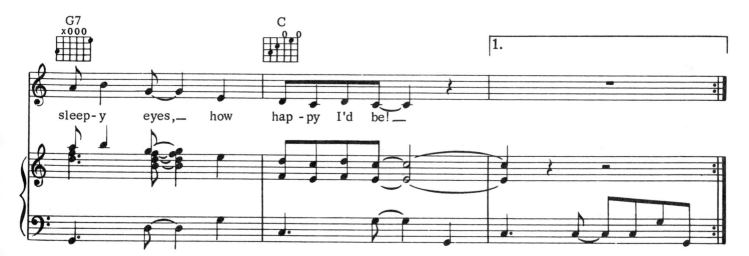

sleep-y eyes,__ how hap-py I'd be!__

1.

some sweet day,_ gon-na take a-way_ this hurt-in' in-side._

Well, I'll nev-er be blue,_ my dreams come true,_____

on Blue Bay -

ou. _____

JUST BECAUSE

Words and Music by
MICHAEL O'HARA, ALEX BROWN
and SAMI McKINNEY

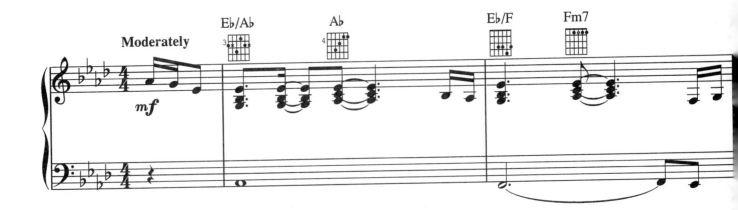

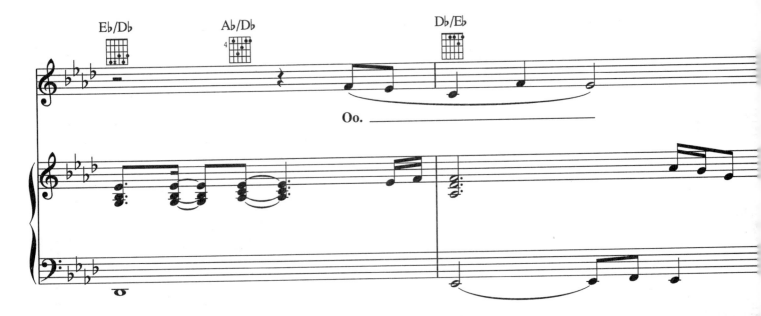

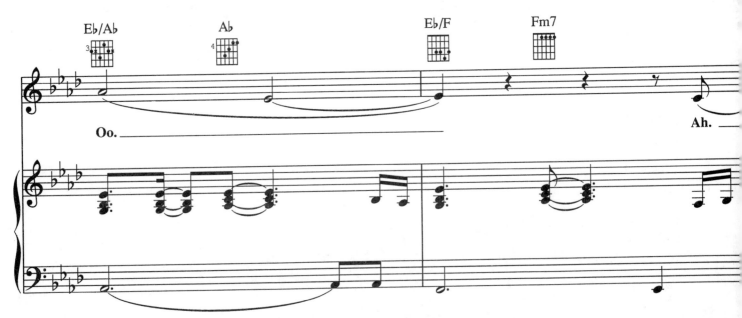

Just Because - 7 - 1

FOR YOUR EYES ONLY

Lyrics by
MICHAEL LEESON

Music by
BILL CONTI

For Your Eyes Only - 3 - 1

42

THE ROSE

Words and Music by
AMANDA McBROOM

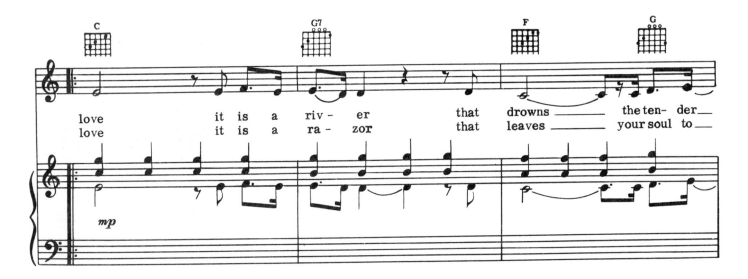

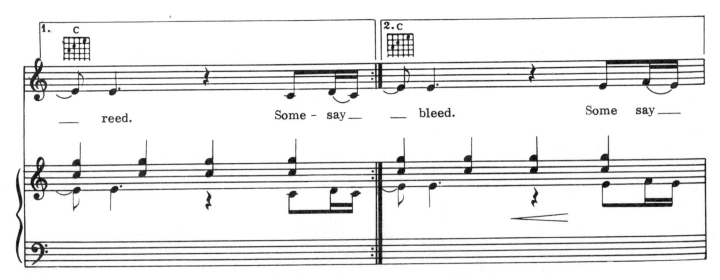

The Rose - 4 - 1

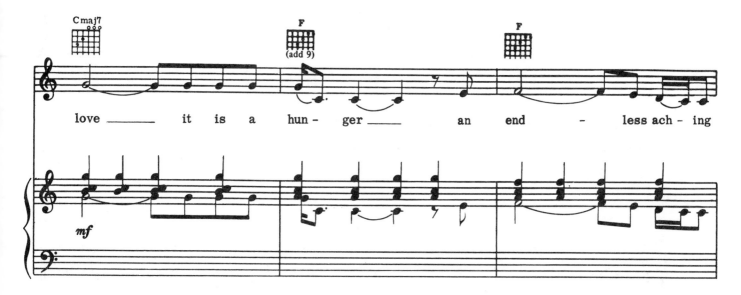

love _____ it is a hun - ger _____ an end ---- less ach - ing

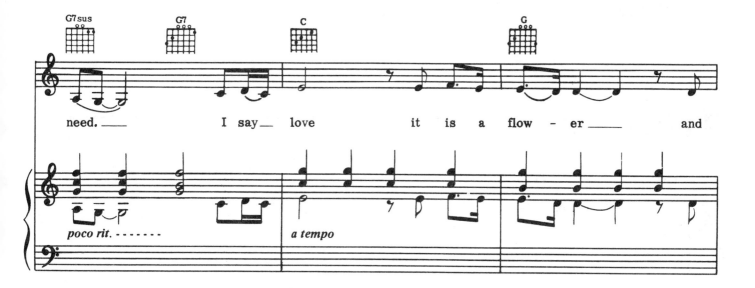

need. ____ I say ___ love it is a flow - er _____ and

you it's on - ly seed. _____ It's the __

GET HERE

Words and Music by
BRENDA RUSSELL

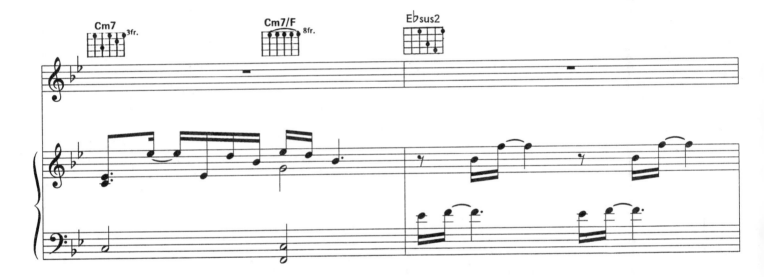

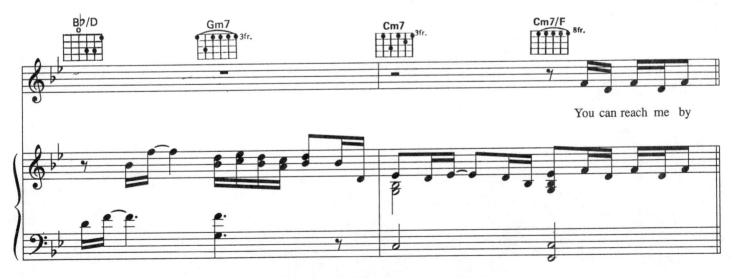

You can reach me by

52

STRONG ENOUGH

Words and Music by
MARK TAYLOR and
PAUL BARRY

Moderate dance ♩ = 132   *Verse 1:*

1. I don't need _____ your sym - pa - thy, there's noth - ing you can say or do _____ for me. And I don't _____ want a mir - a - cle. You'll nev - er change _____ for no _____ one.

56

___ your__ breath__ and walk___ a - way. No mat - ter what__ I hear__

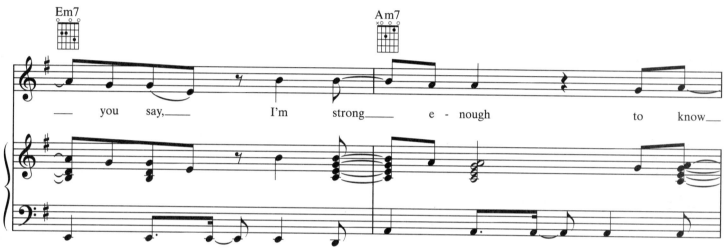

___ you say,___ I'm strong___ e - nough to know___

Repeat ad lib. and fade

___ you've___ got - ta go._____ 'Cause I'm strong___

WHAT'S LOVE GOT TO DO WITH IT

Words and Music by
TERRY BRITTEN and GRAHAM LYLE

What's Love Got to Do With It - 5 - 4

Verse 2:
It may seem to you
That I'm acting confused
When you're close to me.
If I tend to look dazed,
I read it some place;
I've got cause to be.
There's a name for it,
There's a phrase that fits,
But whatever the reason,
You do it for me.

(To Chorus)

HOPELESSLY DEVOTED TO YOU

Words and Music by
JOHN FARRAR

Guess mine is not the first_____ heart
know I'm just a fool_____ who's
head is say - in', "Fool,_____ for -

bro - ken._____ My eyes are not the first_____ to cry.
will - in'_____ to sit a - round and wait_____ for you.
get him."_____ My heart is say - in', "Don't_____ let go.

Hopelessly Devoted to You - 4 - 1

I STILL BELIEVE

Words and Music by
ANTONINA ARMATO
and BEPPE CANTORELLI

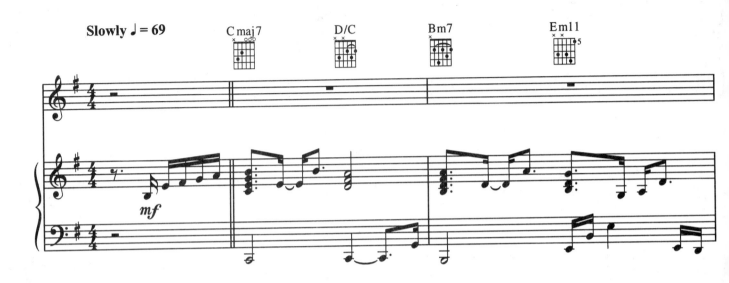

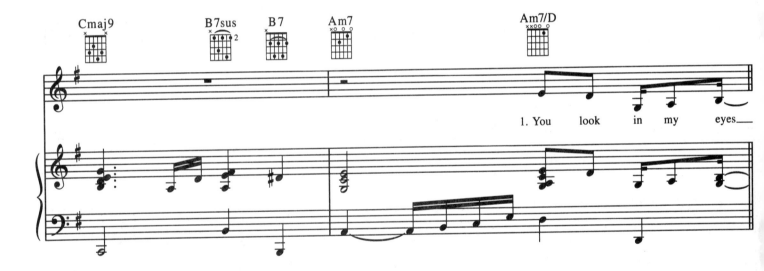

Verse 1:

and I get e-mo-tion-al_____ in-side._____ I know it's

I Still Believe - 6 - 1

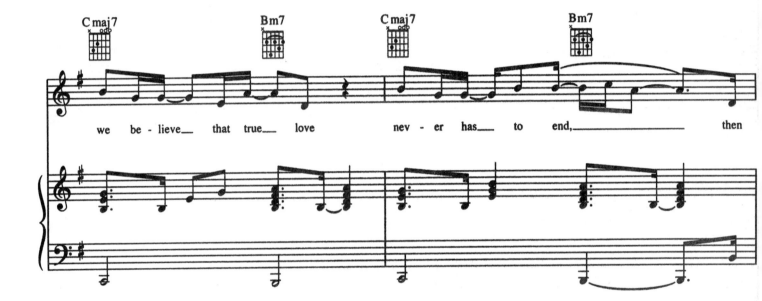

Chorus:

CONSTANT CRAVING

Words and Music by
k.d. lang and BEN MINK

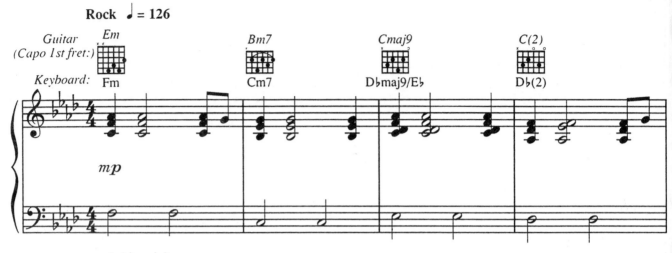

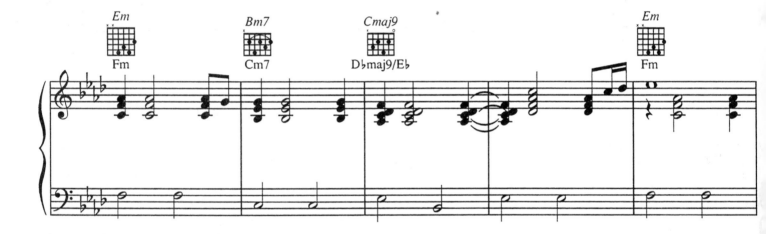

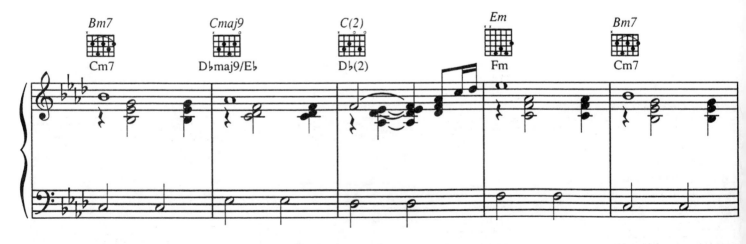

Constant Craving - 4 - 1

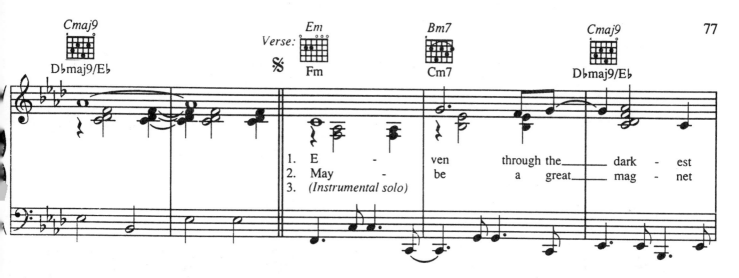

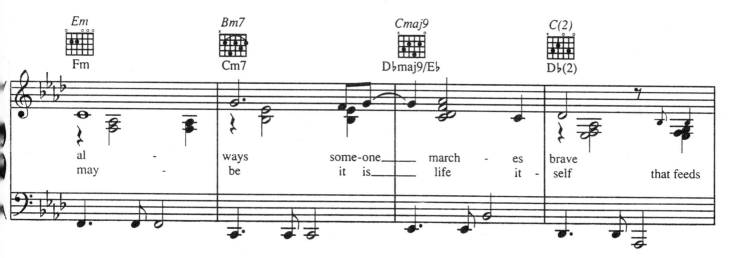

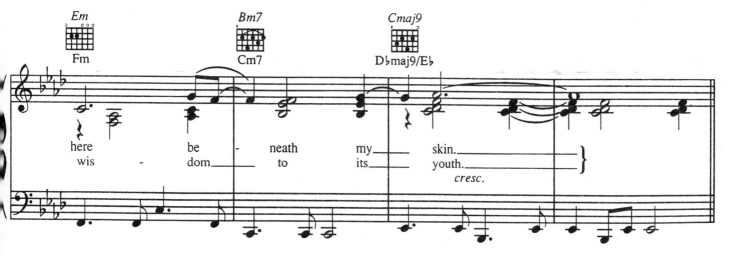

Constant Craving - 4 - 2

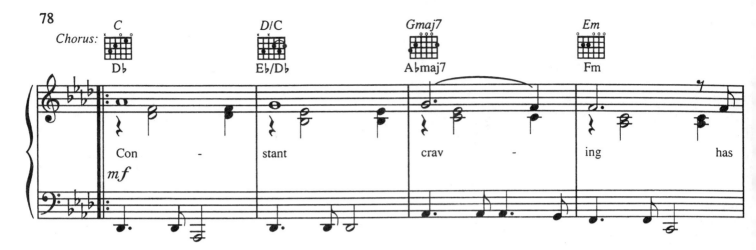

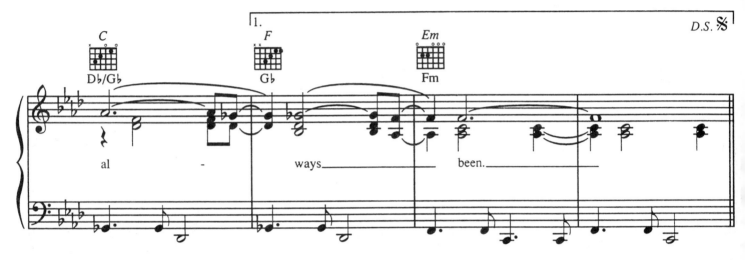

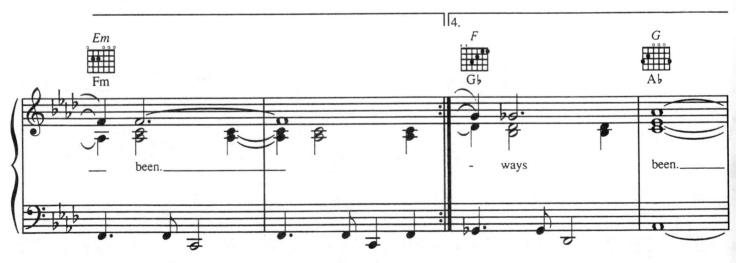

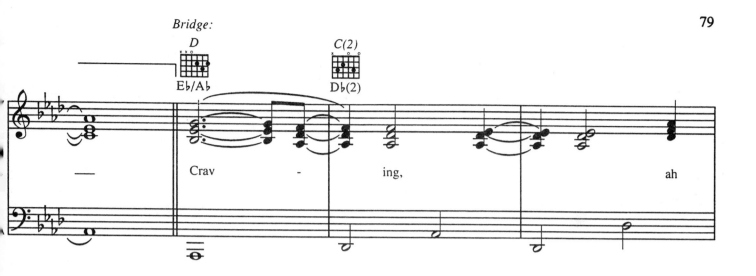

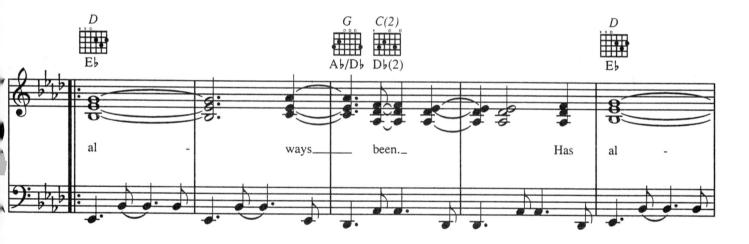

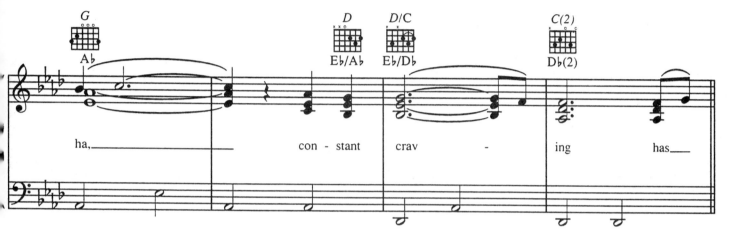

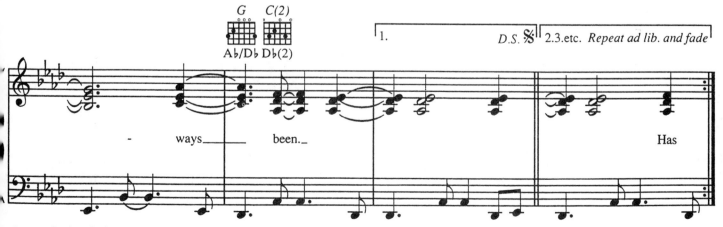

Constant Craving - 4 - 4

CAN'T FIGHT THE MOONLIGHT
(Theme from Coyote Ugly)

Words and Music by
DIANE WARREN

Moderately slow ♩ = 98

Verse:

1. Un - der a lov - er's sky, gon - na be with you, and no
2. There's no es - cape from love. Once the gen - tle breeze

one's gon - na be a - round. If you think that you won't fall, we'll just wait
its spell up - on your heart, no mat - ter what you think, it won't be

Can't Fight the Moonlight - 5 - 2

Bridge:

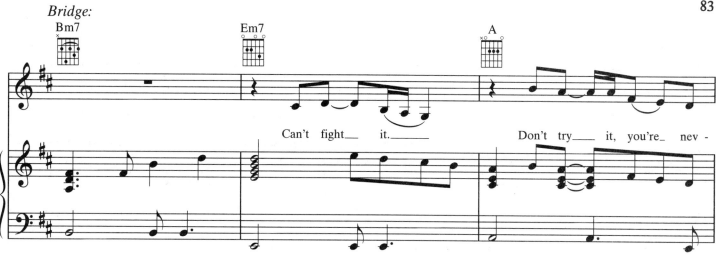

Can't fight___ it.___ Don't try___ it, you're_ nev -

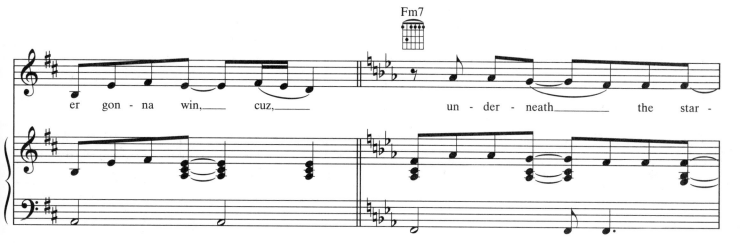

er gon - na win,___ cuz,___ un - der - neath___ the star -

light, star - light,___ there's a mag - i - cal feel - ing so___ right.

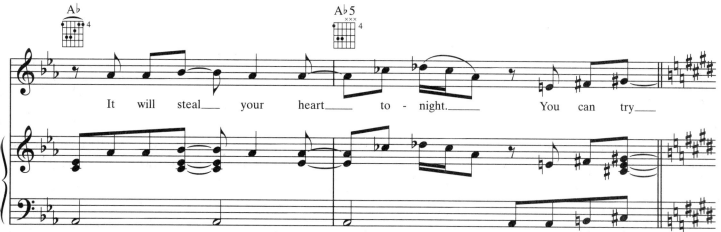

It will steal___ your heart___ to - night.___ You can try___

Can't Fight the Moonlight - 5 - 4

84

From the Motion Picture AUSTIN POWERS: The Spy Who Shagged Me

BEAUTIFUL STRANGER

Words and Music by
MADONNA CICCONE and WILLIAM ORBIT

1. Have-n't we met?

You're some kind of beau-ti-ful strang-er. You could be good

Chorus:

To Coda ⊕

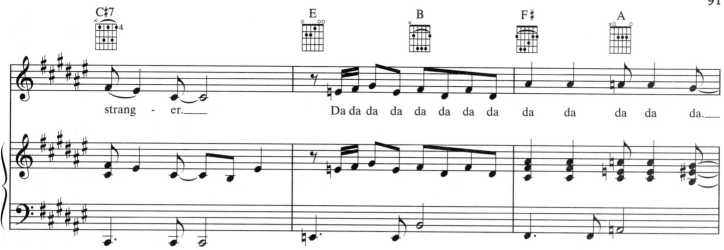

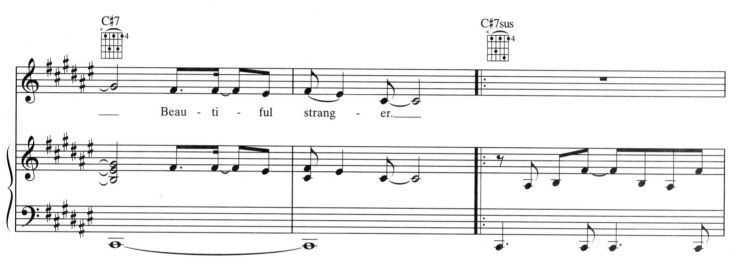

THAT'S THE WAY

Words and Music by
HOLLY LAMAR and ANNIE ROBOFF

Verse:

1. Ev-'ry-bod-y wants an eas-y ride_ on the mer-ry-go-round that we_ call life.
2. *See additional lyrics*

Take a drive on cruise con-trol,_ then you wake to find_ it's a wind-ing road.

That's the Way - 4 - 1

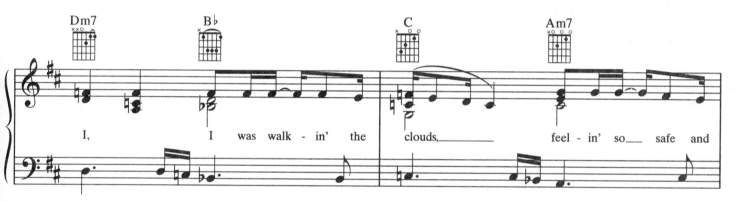

That's the Way - 4 - 2

That's the way__ it goes;__ you got-ta bend when the wind blows.

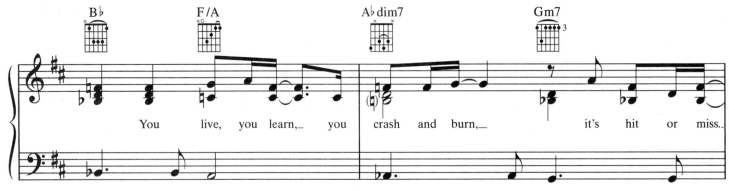

You live, you learn,__ you crash and burn,__ it's hit or miss.

To Coda ⊕ 1.

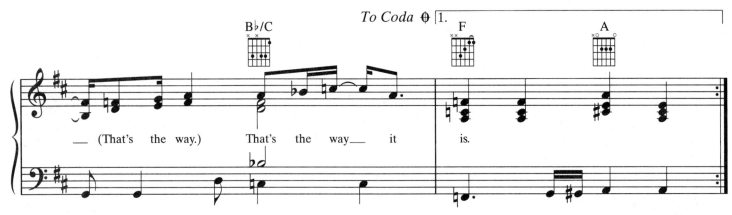

__ (That's the way.) That's the way__ it is.

2.   *Bridge:*

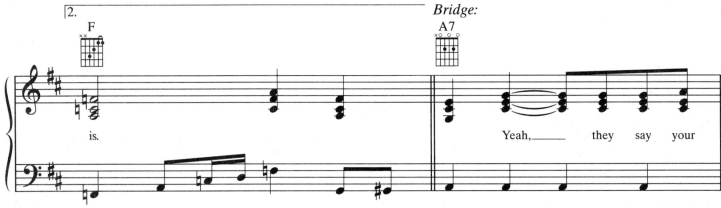

is.   Yeah,____ they say your

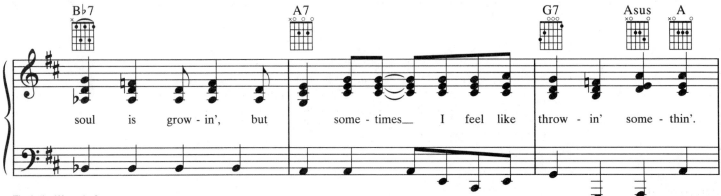

soul is grow-in', but some-times__ I feel like throw-in' some-thin'.

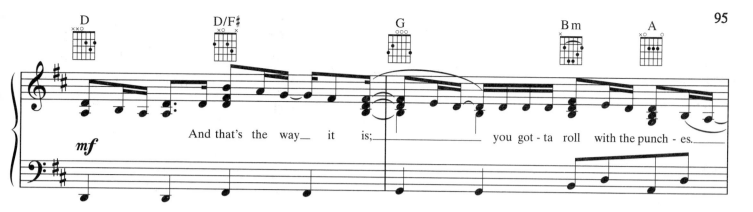

Verse 2:
One fine day you wake up, completely hopelessly fallin' in love.
He's just what you're lookin' for; the only problem is that the man's not sure.
Another guy'll give you everything; only problem is, you don't feel a thing.
Well, I know from experience, nothing's ever gonna make perfect sense.
Oh, one day you get what you want, but it's not what you think.
Then you get what you need.
(To Chorus:)

From the New Line Cinema Motion Picture "SET IT OFF"

DON'T LET GO (LOVE)

Words and Music by
ANDREA MARTIN, IVAN MATIAS,
MARQUEZE ETHERIDGE and ORGANIZED NOIZE

Don't Let Go (Love) - 5 - 1

98

Love mak - ing, heart - break - ing, soul___ shak - ing.___ What's it gon - na

Chorus:

be, 'cause I___ can't pre - tend?___ Don't you wan - na be more___ than friends?___

___ Then hold me tight and don't let go,___ don't___ let go.___ We have the right to lose con -

trol.___ Don't___ let go.___

I LOVE YOU ALWAYS FOREVER

Words and Music by
DONNA LEWIS

"I Love You Always Forever" is inspired by the H.E. Bates novel "Love for Lydia."
Chorus/Bridge lyric courtesy of *Michael Joseph Ltd.* and *The Estate of H.E. Bates.*

Love You Always Forever - 5 - 1

Verse 3:
You've got the most unbelievable blue eyes I've ever seen.
You've got me almost melting away as we lay there
Under blue sky with pure white stars,
Exotic sweetness, a magical time.
(To Chorus:)

NOBODY DOES IT BETTER

Lyrics by
CAROLE BAYER SAGER

Music by
MARVIN HAMLISCH

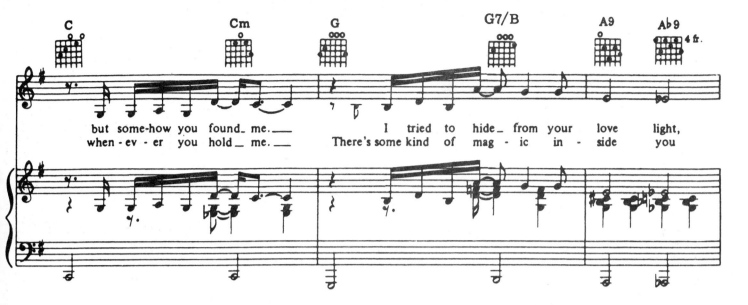

but some-how you found_ me.____ I tried to hide_ from your love light,
when-ev-er you hold_ me.____ There's some kind of mag-ic in-side you

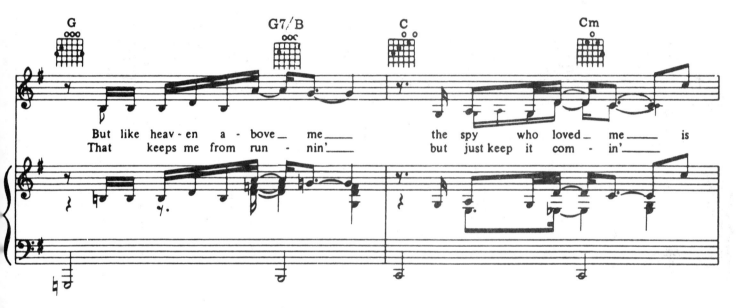

But like heav-en a-bove_ me____ the spy who loved_ me____ is
That keeps me from run-nin'____ but just keep it com-in'____

keep-in' all my se-crets safe to-night.
how'd you learn to do the things you do? And

FOR YOU I WILL

Words and Music by
DIANE WARREN

Verse:

1. When you're feel-ing lost in the night,___ when you feel your
heart from the rain,___ I won't let no

world just ain't right,_____ call on me,___ I will___ be wait-ing. Count on me,___
harm come your way._____ Oh, these arms___ will be___ your shel-ter, no, these arms_

For You I Will - 5 - 1

Chorus:

From the Touchstone Motion Picture "CON AIR"

HOW DO I LIVE

Words and Music by
DIANE WARREN

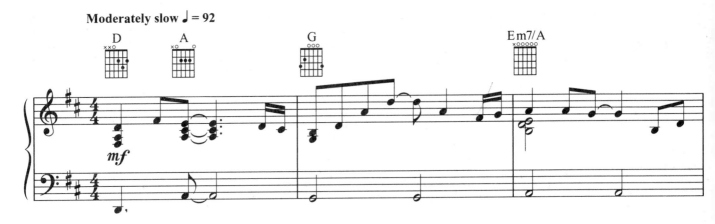

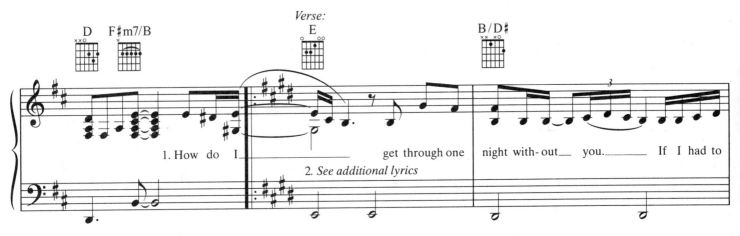

1. How do I_____ get through one night with-out__ you.____ If I had to

2. *See additional lyrics*

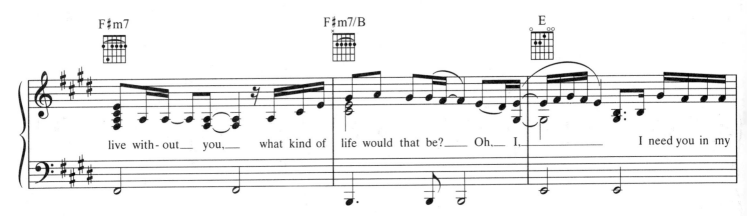

live with-out__ you,__ what kind of life would that be?__ Oh,__ I,__ I need you in my

arms, need you__ to hold.__ You're my world, my heart,__ my soul.__ If you ev-er leave,____

How Do I Live - 4 - 1

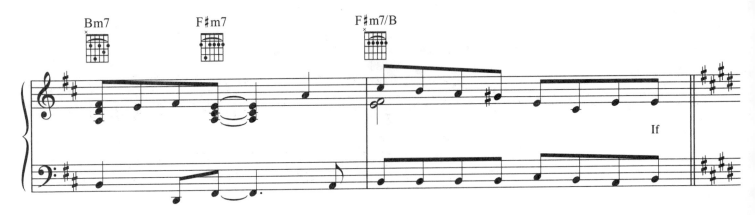

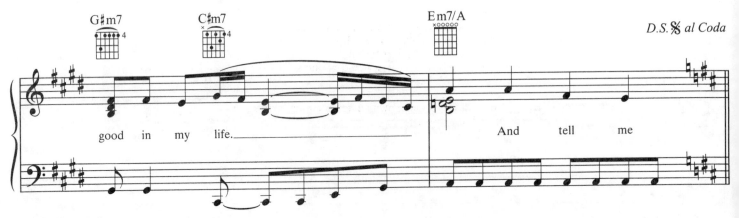

now how do I, oh, how do I live

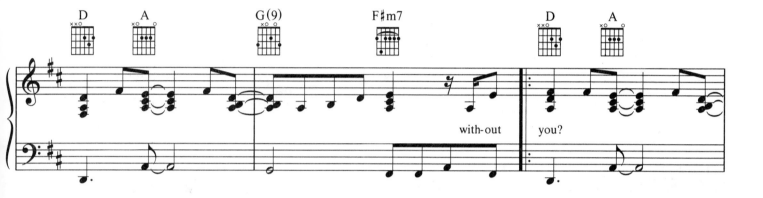

with-out you?

*Repeat ad lib. and fade
(vocal 1st time only)*

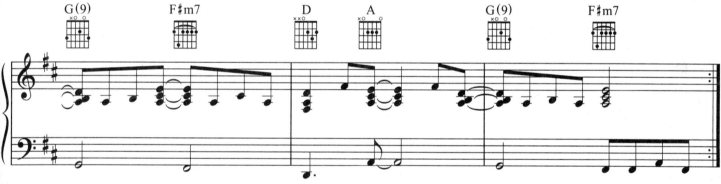

Verse 2:
Without you, there'd be no sun in my sky,
There would be no love in my life,
There'd be no world left for me.
And I, baby, I don't know what I would do,
I'd be lost if I lost you.
If you ever leave,
Baby, you would take away everything real in my life.
And tell me now...
(To Chorus:)

OUT HERE ON MY OWN

Lyrics by
LESLIE GORE

Music by
MICHAEL GORE

Out Here on My Own - 3 - 1

PEOPLE

Words by
BOB MERRILL

Music by
JULE STYNE

122

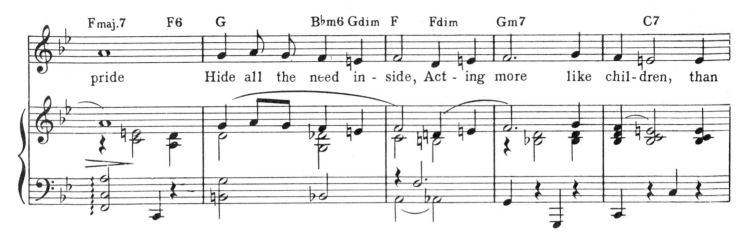

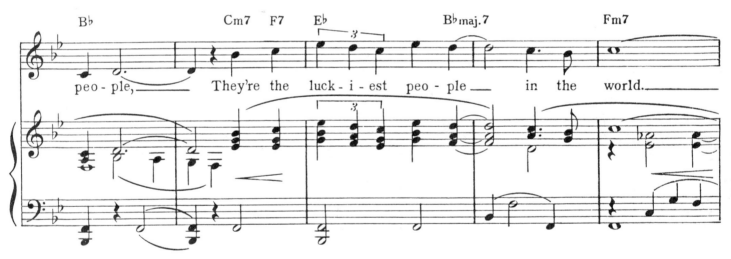

People - 3 - 2

deep in your soul ___ Says: you were half, now you're whole.___ No more

hun - ger and thirst, But first, be a per - son who needs peo - ple.___

___ Peo - ple who need peo - ple ___ Are the luck - i - est peo - ple in the

world. ___   world. ___

People - 3 - 3

PIANO IN THE DARK

Words and Music by
BRENDA RUSSELL, JEFF HULL
and SCOTT CUTLER

When I find my-self watch-in' the time,___

Piano in the Dark - 5 - 1

126

I think of let-ting go. Oh,___ no,___ gave up on the rid-dle, I cry___

___ just a lit-tle when he plays pi-an-o in ___ the dark.

To Coda ⊕

___ the dark.

Oh, the

si - lence is bro - ken and no words are spo - ken. But oh,___

the dark.

THE WAY I WANT TO TOUCH YOU

Words and Music by
TONI TENNILLE

The Way I Want to Touch You - 3 - 1

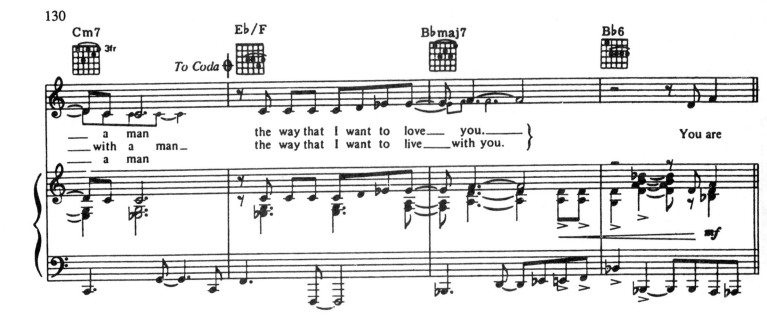

the way that I want to love___ you.___
___ with a man___ the way that I want to live___ with you.
___ a man

You are

sun - shine,___ you are shad - ow;___ you are morn - ing, you are night.___ You are

hard times,___ you are good___ times;___ you are dark - ness, you are___ light.___

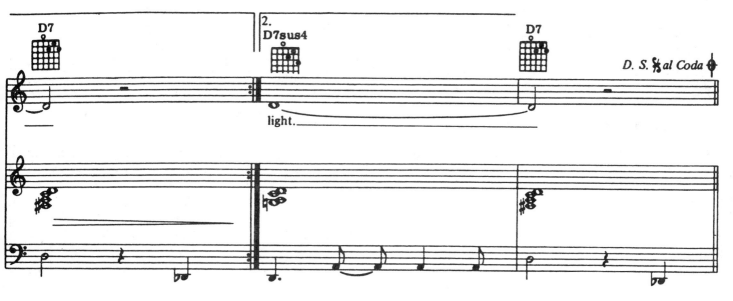

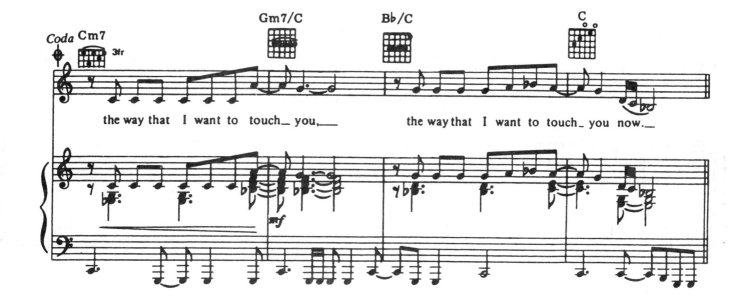

The Way I Want to Touch You - 3 - 3

OOPS!... I DID IT AGAIN

Words and Music by
MAX MARTIN and RAMI

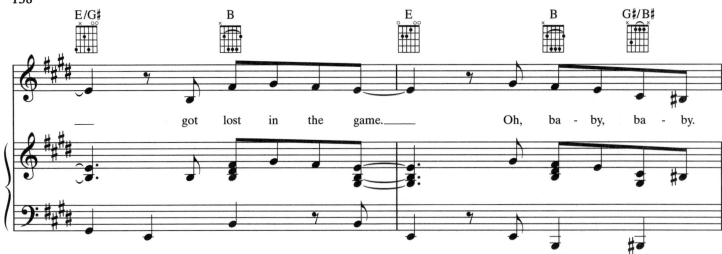

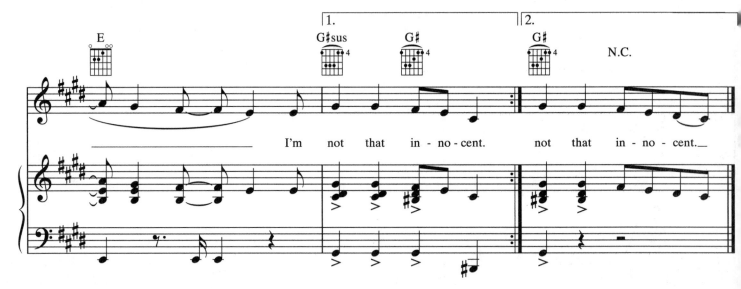

I WANT YOU TO NEED ME

Words and Music by
DIANE WARREN

I Want You to Need Me - 5 - 1

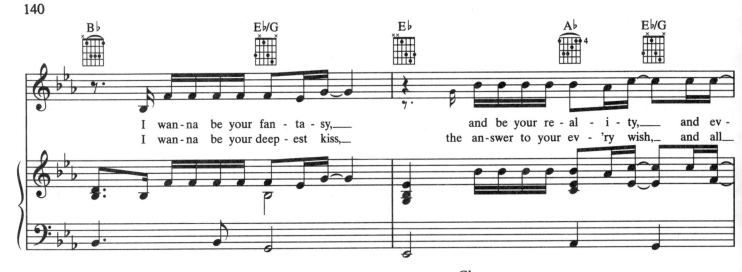

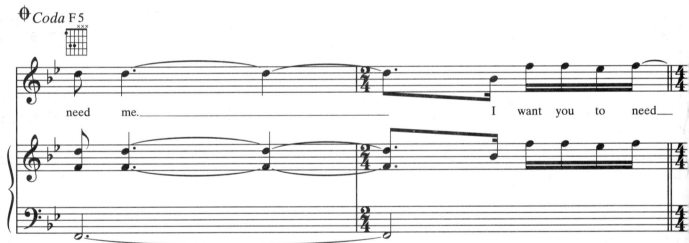

NEW ATTITUDE

Words and Music by
BUNNY HILL, JON GILUTIN and
SHARON T. ROBINSON

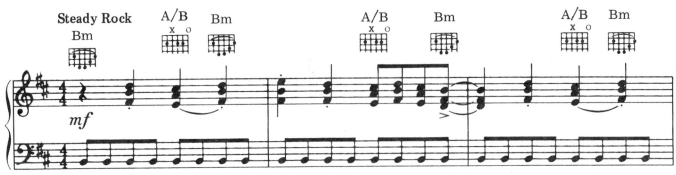

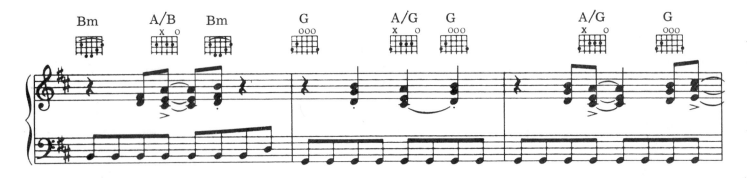

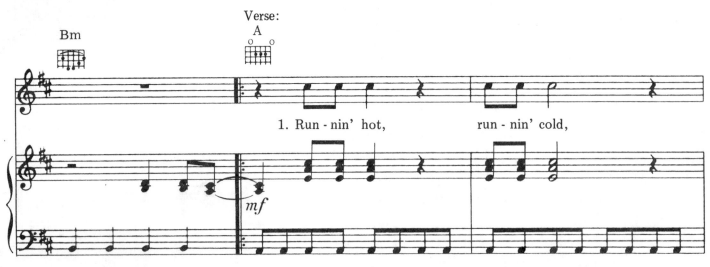

1. Run - nin' hot,   run - nin' cold,

New Attitude - 5 - 1

New Attitude - 5 - 2

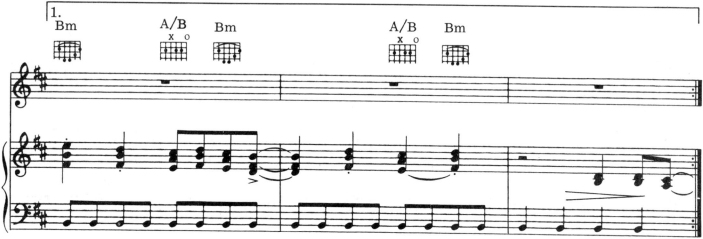

New Attitude - 5 - 4

Verse 2.

I'm wearing a new dress, new hat,
Brand new ideals, as a matter of fact
I'm changed for good.
It must have been a cool night, new moon,
Slight change, or that particular night
That makes me feel like I should.

Somehow the wires uncrossed, the tables were turned,
And then I knew I had such a lesson to learn.
(Chorus)

From the Warner Bros. Motion Picture "ROMEO MUST DIE"

TRY AGAIN

Words and Music by
TIM MOSLEY and STEPHEN "STATIC" GARRETT

Try Again - 5 - 1

you give up or try a - gain if I hes - i - tate to let you in? Now would you
till I see what this could be, could be e - ter - ni - ty or just a week. You know our

be your-self or play a role, tell all the boys or keep it low? If
chem-is - try is off the chain, it's per-fect now, but will it change? This

I say no, would you turn a - way or play me off, or would you stay? } And if at
ain't a yes, this ain't a no. Just do your thing and see how it goes. }

Chorus:

first you don't__ suc - ceed,_____ dust your-self off and try__

Try Again - 5 - 3

Huh? Huh? Huh? Huh? I said you don't wan-na throw it all a-way.___ I might be

D.S. ℅ al Coda

bug-gin' on the first date. What a-bout the next date? Huh? Huh? Huh? Huh? And if at

⊕ Coda

N.C.

___ a-gain,___ try a-gain.

1.

2.

And if at

Chorus:

first you don't___ suc - ceed,_____ dust your-self off and try___ ___ a - gain.___ You can dust it off and try___ a - gain,___ try a - gain. 'Cause if at first you don't___ suc - ceed,_____ you can dust it off and try___ ___ a - gain.___ Dust your-self off and try___ a - gain,___ try a - gain. And if at

Repeat ad lib. and fade

BAG LADY

Words and Music by ISAAC HAYES,
ANDRE YOUNG, BRIAN BAILEY, C. LONGMILES,
RICARDO BROWN, NATHANIEL HALE
and ERYKAH BADU

Bag Lady - 7 - 1

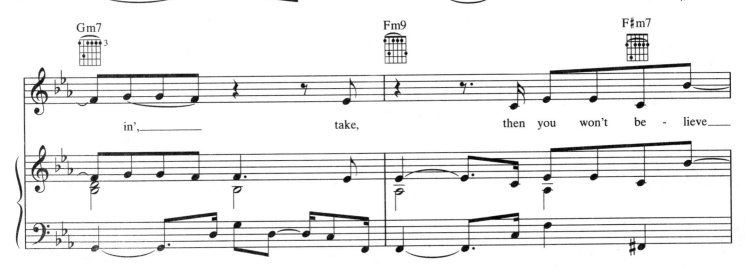

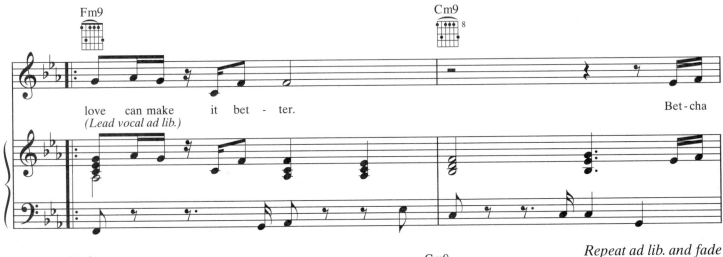

Repeat ad lib. and fade

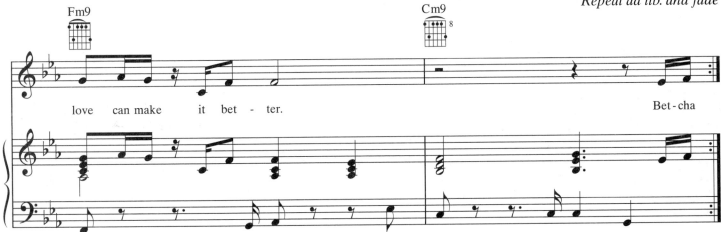

Verse 2:
Bag lady, you gon' miss your bus.
You can't hurry up 'cause you got too much stuff.
When they see you comin', niggas take off runnin'
From you, it's true, oh, yes, they do.
One day, he gon' say, "You crowdin' my space."
One day, he gon' say, "You crowdin' my space."
One day, he gon' say, "You crowdin' my space."
One day, he gon' say, "You crowdin' my space."
(To Chorus:)

Bag Lady - 7 - 7

YOU'RE STILL THE ONE

Words and Music by
SHANIA TWAIN and R.J. LANGE

Slowly ♩ = 72

(Drums only)

(Spoken:) When I first saw you, I saw love.

And the first time you touched me, I felt love. And after all this time,

you're still the one I love.

1. Looks like we made___ it.
2. See additional lyrics

Look how far___ we've come,___ my ba - by.___ We might-a took the long___ way.

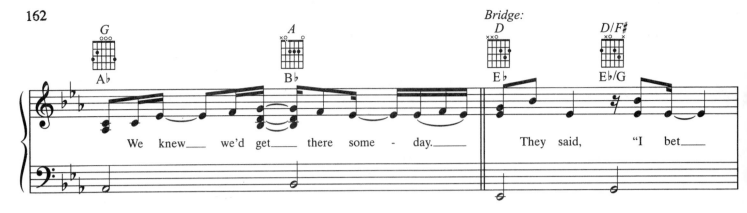

We knew__ we'd get__ there some - day.__ They said, "I bet__

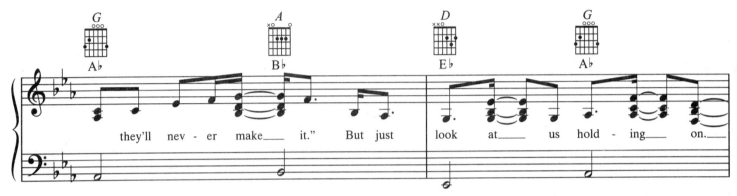

they'll nev - er make__ it." But just look at__ us hold - ing__ on.__

__ We're still to - geth - er, still go - ing__ strong.__

% *Chorus:*

__ (You're still the one.__) You're still the one I run__ to,

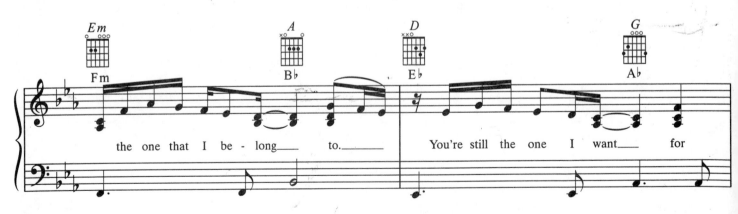

the one that I be - long__ to.__ You're still the one I want__ for

Verse 2:
Ain't nothin' better,
We beat the odds together.
I'm glad we didn't listen.
Look at what we would be missin'.
(To Bridge:)

You're Still the One - 3 - 3

UN-BREAK MY HEART

Words and Music by
DIANE WARREN

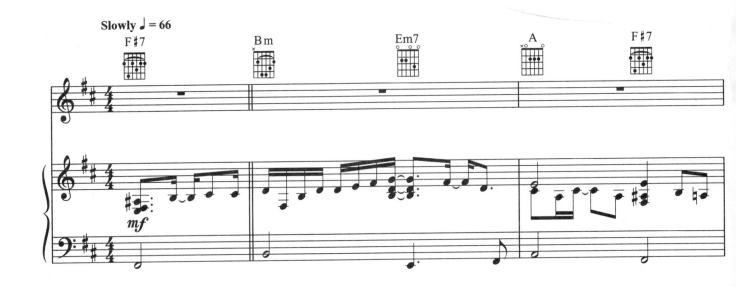

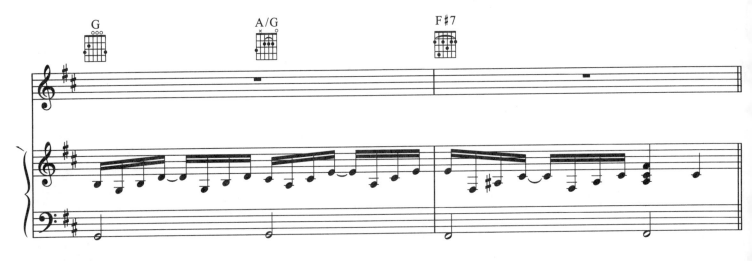

Verse:

1. Don't leave me in___ all this pain,___ don't leave me out___ in the rain.___
2. Take back that sad___ word good-bye,___ bring back the joy___ to my life.___

Un-Break My Heart - 5 - 1

%% Chorus:

168

C
A7
Dm
Gm7
Come back and say you love me.
Un - break my heart, sweet dar - ling.
Without you, I just can't go on.
Repeat ad lib. and fade

From the Motion Picture DOGMA

STILL

Words and Music by
ALANIS MORISSETTE

Tune Guitar:
⑥ = D ③ = G
⑤ = A ② = B
④ = D ① = D

Slowly ♩ = 74

1. I am the harm that you in - flict.
4. I am your trag - e - dy and your for - tune.

I am your bril - liance and your frus - tra - tion.
I am your cri - sis and your de - light.

*Original recording in D♭.

Still - 7 - 1

Verses 2, 3, & 5:

2. I am your mis - fits and your prais - ed.___
3. I am your joy and your re - gret.
5. I am your death and your de - ci - sions.___

I am your doubt and your con - vic - tion.
I am your fu - ry and your e - la - tion.
I am your pas - sion and your plights.

I'm the nu - cle - ar bombs if they're to hit.
I am your proph - ets and your prof - its.

I am your im - ma - tur - i - ty and your in - di - gence.
I am your art, I am your bytes.

Ah._____

Ah._____

D.S. % al Coda

Ah._____

Coda

B♭maj7   C   D   Em7

And I love you   still._____

I see you_____   lie to your coun -

174

Ah.

Ah.

Ah.

Repeat ad lib. and fade

*First time only.

TOGETHER AGAIN

Words and Music by
JANET JACKSON, JAMES HARRIS III,
TERRY LEWIS and RENÉ ELIZONDO, JR.

Moderately fast ♩ = 120

Together Again - 7 - 1

Danc-in' in moon-light.___ I know you are_ free.___ 'cause I can see your_ star_

1.
___ shin-in' down on_ me.

2.
___ shin-in' down on_ me.___

N.C.

Repeat ad lib. and fade

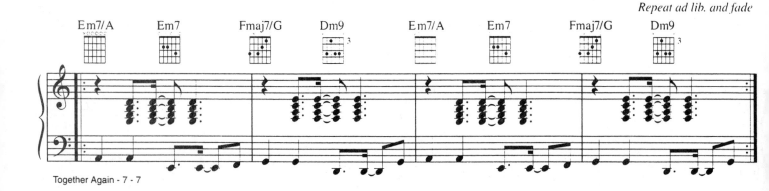

Together Again - 7 - 7

EX-GIRLFRIEND

Words and Music by
GWEN STEFANI, TOM DUMONT
and TONY KANAL

Fast rock ♩ = 168

Chorus:

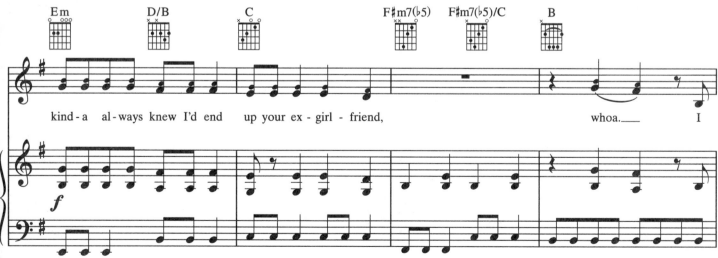

kind-a al-ways knew I'd end up your ex-girl-friend, whoa.___ I

Ex-Girlfriend - 9 - 1

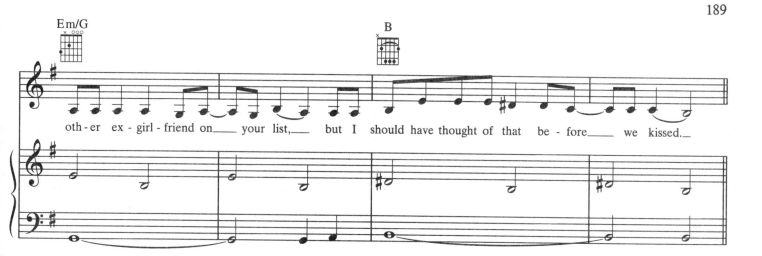

oth-er ex-girl-friend on____ your list,____ but I should have thought of that be-fore____ we kissed.____

N.C.

I'm a-bout to

Bridge:

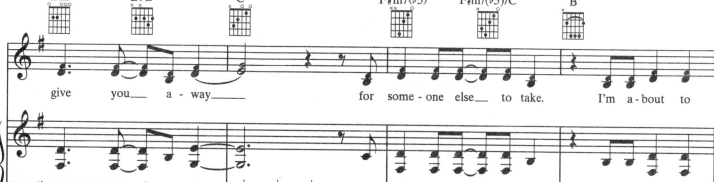

give you____ a-way____ for some-one else____ to take. I'm a-bout to

Ex-Girlfriend - 9 - 7

I SAY A LITTLE PRAYER

Words by
HAL DAVID

Music by
BURT BACHARACH

Say a lit-tle prayer for you,___ I say a lit-tle prayer for you.___

Verse:

1. The mo-ment I wake___ up,___ be-fore I put
2. I run___ for the bus,___ dear, while rid-ing I

Chorus:

ev - er, for - ev - er, you'll stay in my heart___ and I will love you. For -

ev - er and ev - er, we nev - er will part,___ oh, how I'll love you. To -

geth - er, to - geth - er, that's how it should be.___ To live with - out you would

on - ly mean heart - break for me.

Chorus:

I TURN TO YOU

Words and Music by
DIANE WARREN

2. When I lose___

2. to car - ry on,_____ for

ev - 'ry - thing___ you do,___ I turn to you.___

Bridge:

For the arms to be___ my shel - ter through all the rain,___ for

Chorus:

I WILL LOVE AGAIN

Words and Music by
PAUL BARRY and MARK TAYLOR

Moderately fast ♩ = 128

Verse:

1. Did I ev - er tell you how you live____ in me ev - 'ry wak - ing mo - ment, e - ven in__ my dreams?__ And if all this talk__ is cra-
2. Peo - ple nev - er tell you the way they real - ly feel. I would die for you__ glad - ly if I knew it was__ for real. So if all this talk__ sounds cra-

I will love___ a - gain___

To Coda ⊕

e - ven if it takes a life - time to___ get o - ver you.

1.

Heav - en on - ly knows___ I will love a -

gain.___

I WILL SURVIVE

Words and Music by
FREDERICK J. PERREN and DINO FEKARIS

I Will Survive - 5 - 1

INSEPARABLE

Words and Music by
CHARLES JACKSON and
MARVIN JEROME YANCY

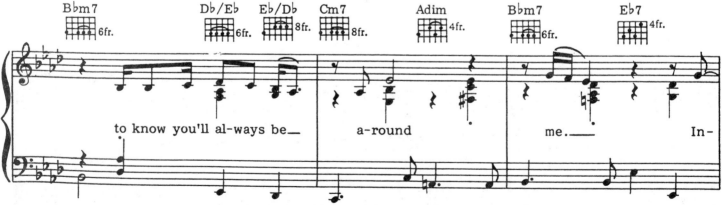

Inseparable - 4 - 1

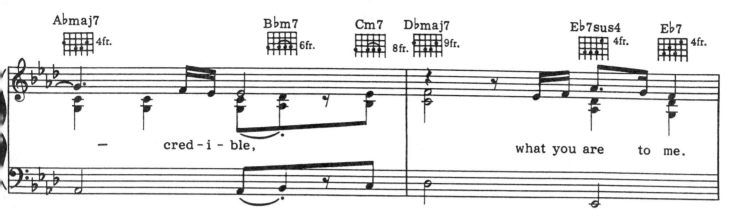

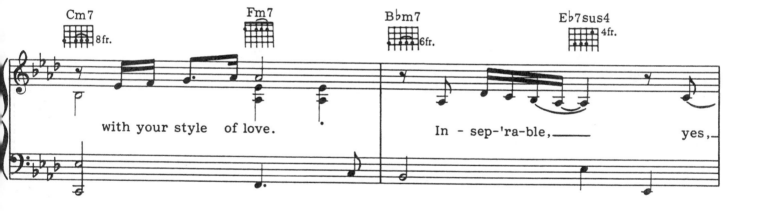

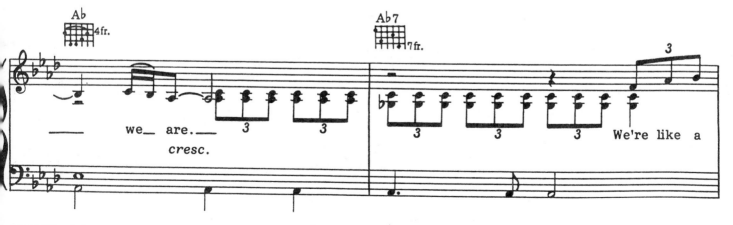

Inseparable - 4 - 2

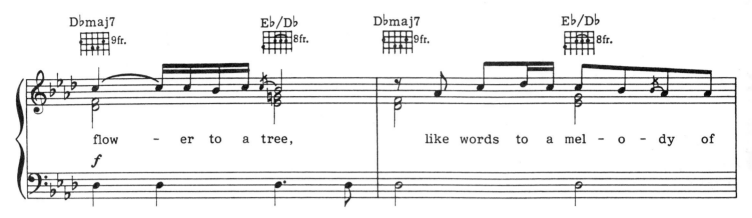

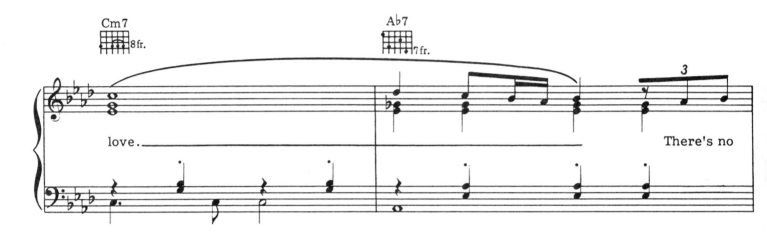

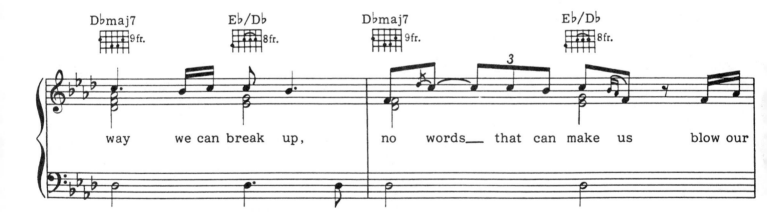

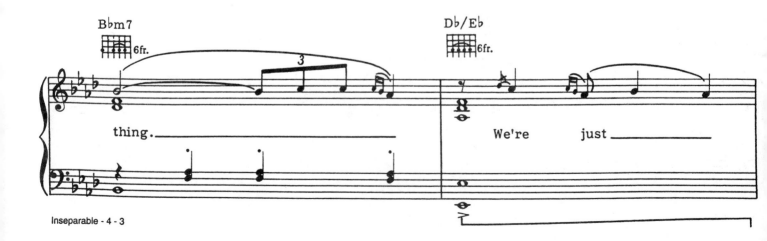

Inseparable - 4 - 3

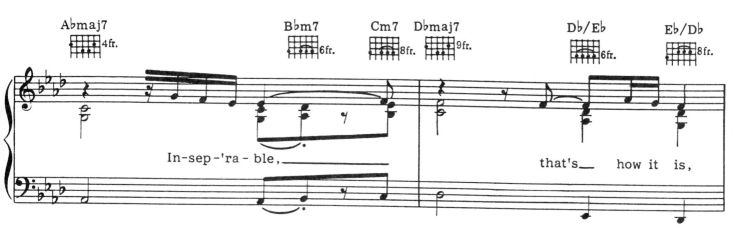

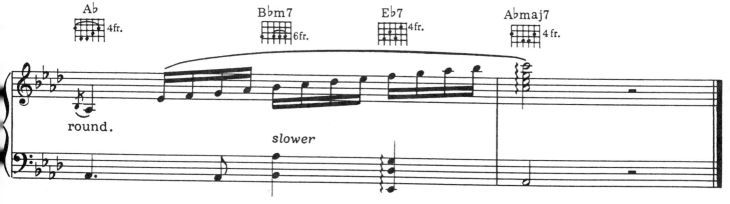

From The Fox Searchlight Film, "THE BROTHERS McMULLEN"

I WILL REMEMBER YOU

Words and Music by
SARAH McLACHLAN, SEAMUS EGAN
and DAVE MERENDA

I Will Remember You - 4 - 1

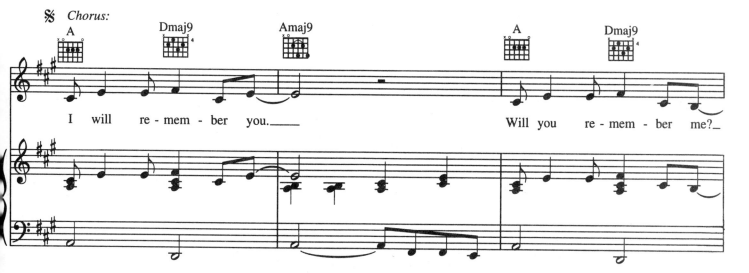

Don't let your life___ pass___ you by,___

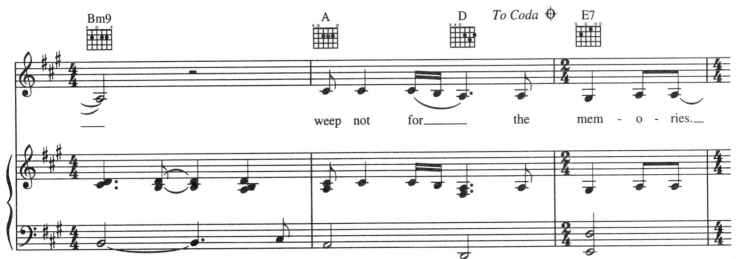

weep not for_____ the mem - o - ries.___

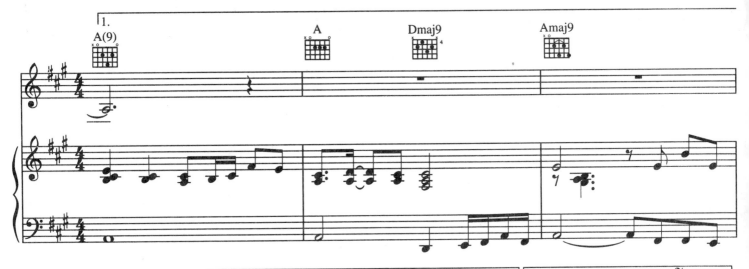

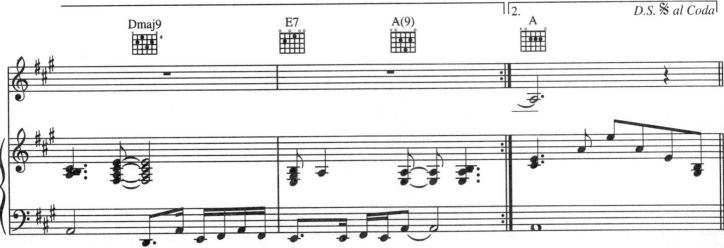

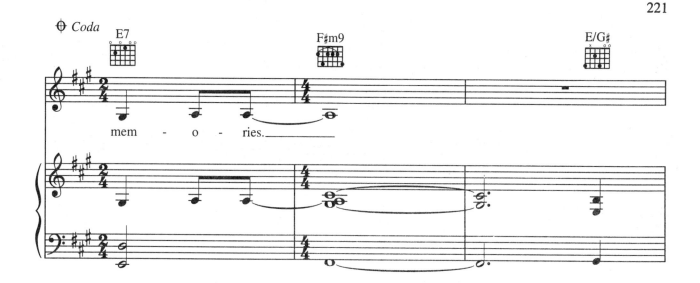

Verse 2:
So afraid to love you,
More afraid to lose.
I'm clinging to a past
That doesn't let me choose.
Where once there was a darkness,
A deep and endless night,
You gave me everything you had,
Oh, you gave me life.
(To Chorus:)

(Optional Verse 1 — Album version)
Remember the good times that we had,
I let them slip away from us when things got bad.
Now clearly I first saw you smiling in the sun.
I wanna feel your warmth upon me,
I wanna be the one.
(To Chorus:)

MacARTHUR PARK

Words and Music by
JIMMY WEBB

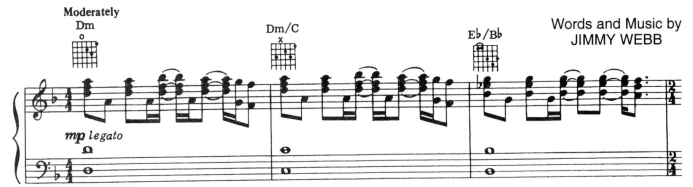

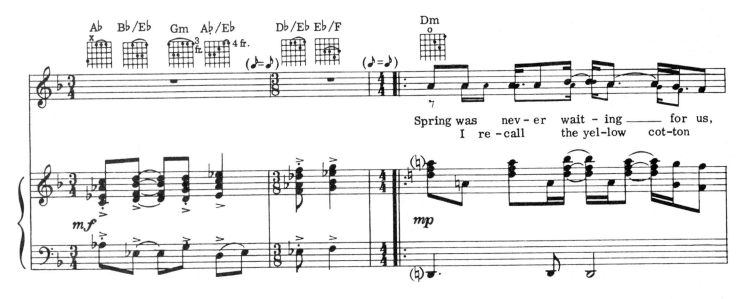

Spring was nev-er wait-ing for us,
I re-call the yel-low cot-ton

girl, it ran one step a-head as we fol-lowed in the
dress foam-ing like a wave on the ground a-round your

MacArthur Park - 10 - 1

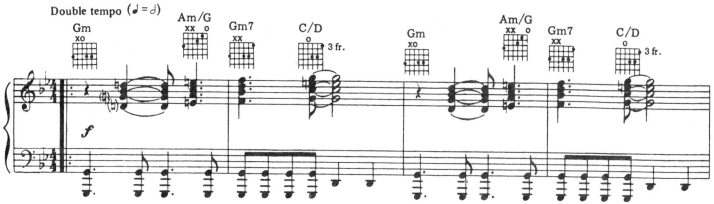

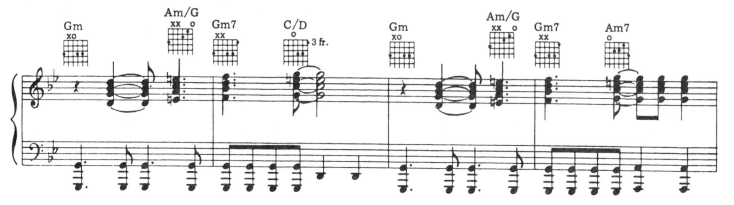

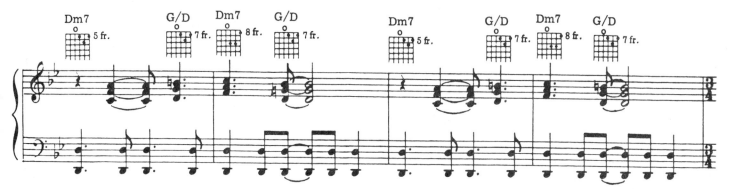

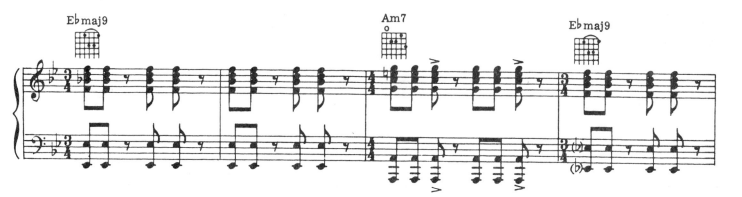

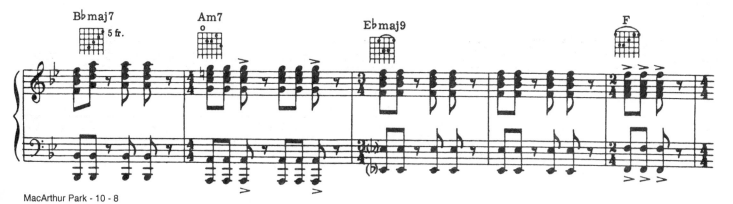

MacArthur Park - 10 - 8

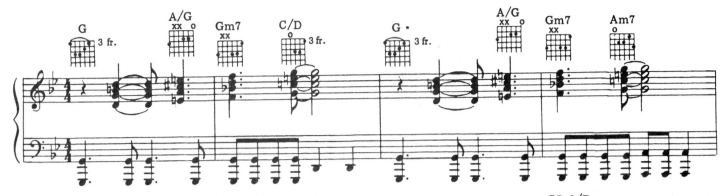

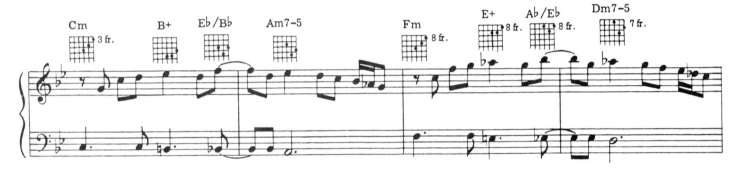

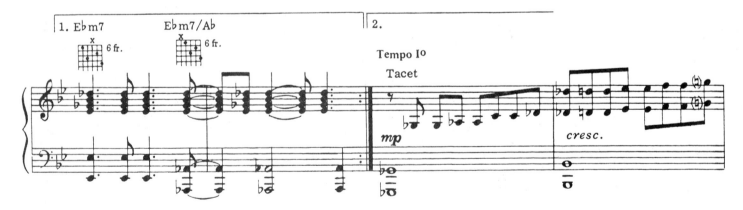

Mac - Ar-thur's Park is melt-ing in the dark, all the sweet green ic-ing

From the Miramax Motion Picture BOUNCE

NEED TO BE NEXT TO YOU

Words and Music by
DIANE WARREN

234

OVER THE RAINBOW

Lyric by
E.Y. HARBURG

Music by
HAROLD ARLEN

From the Universal Motion Picture "CASPER"

REMEMBER ME THIS WAY

Lyrics by
LINDA THOMPSON

Music by
DAVID FOSTER

Remember Me This Way - 6 - 1

SAVE THE BEST FOR LAST

Words and Music by
WENDY WALDMAN, JON LIND
and PHIL GALDSTON

248

THEME FROM ICE CASTLES
(Through the Eyes of Love)

Lyrics by
CAROLE BAYER SAGER

Music by
MARVIN HAMLISCH

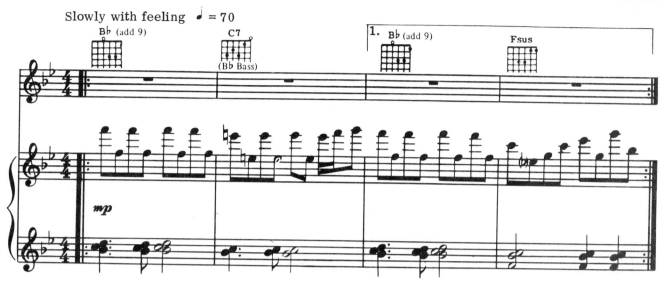

1. Please,   don't let this feel - ing
2. now   I can take the
3. Please,   don't let this feel - ing

(cross hands)

end.   It's ev-'ry-thing I am,   ev-'ry-thing I want   to be.
time.   I can see my life   as it comes up shin - ing now.
end.   It might not come a - gain and I want to re - mem - ber

Theme From Ice Castles - 3 - 1

now I do be-lieve that e-ven in the storm we'll find _____ some

light.   Know-ing you're be-side me I'm all_ right. _____

D.S. al Coda

Coda

through the eyes _____ of love.

Theme From Ice Castles - 3 - 3

SUNNY CAME HOME

Words and Music by
SHAWN COLVIN and JOHN LEVENTHAL

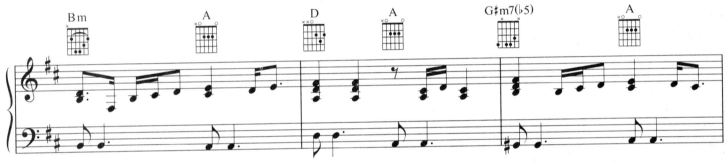

Sunny Came Home - 6 - 1

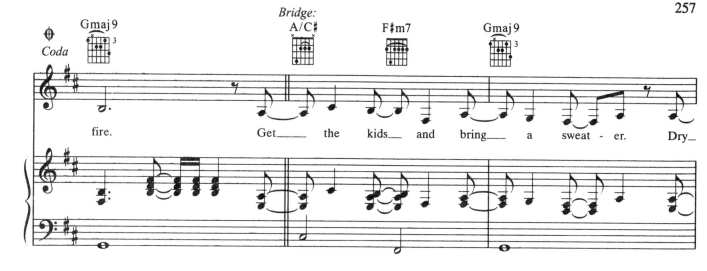

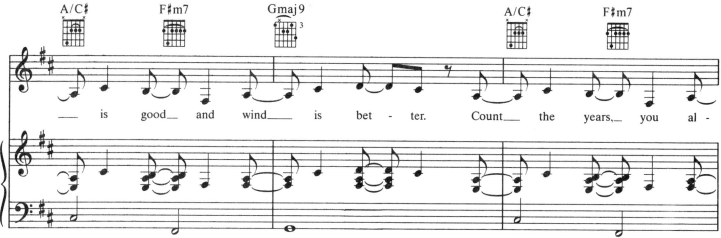

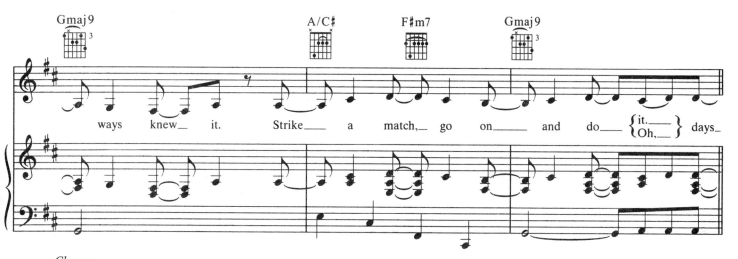

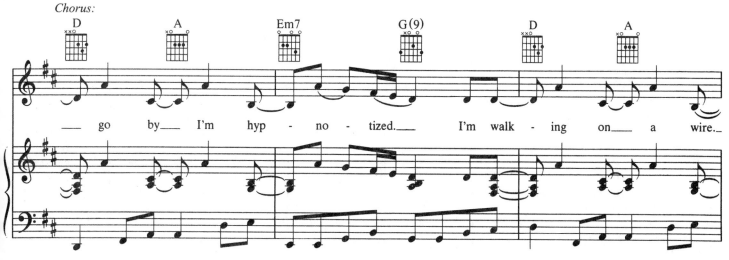

Coda

fire. Get___ the kids___ and bring___ a sweat-er. Dry___

___ is good___ and wind___ is bet-ter. Count___ the years,___ you al-

ways knew___ it. Strike___ a match,___ go on___ and do___ {it.___ / Oh,___} days___

Chorus:

___ go by___ I'm hyp-no-tized.___ I'm walk-ing on___ a wire.___

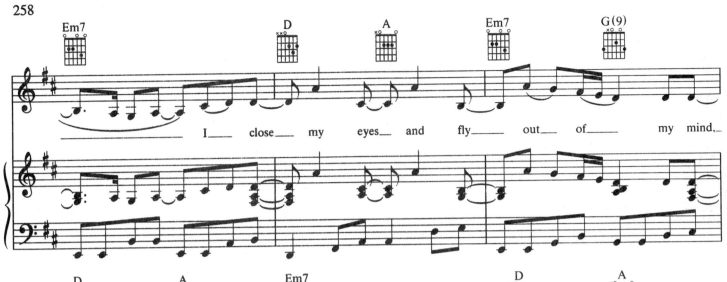

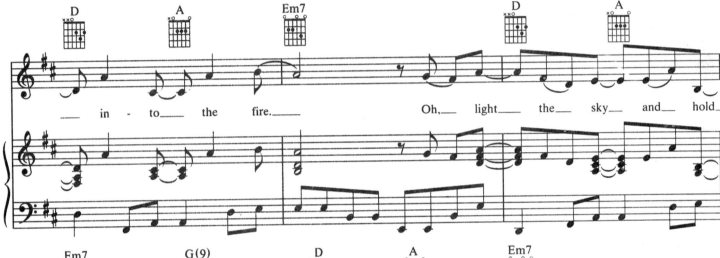

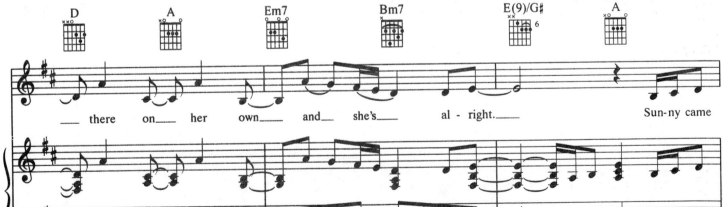

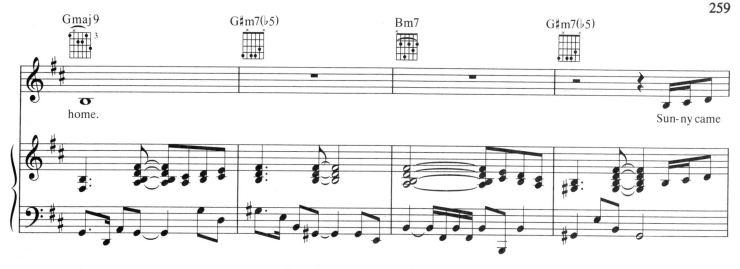

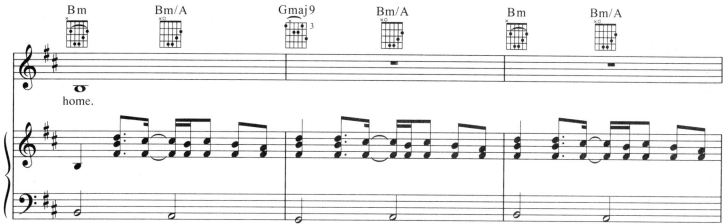

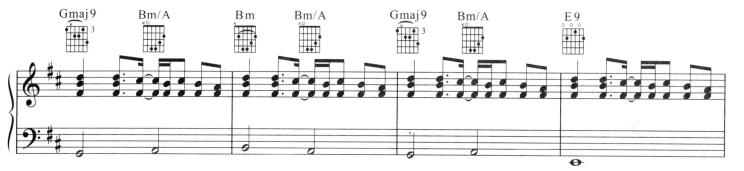

THIS KISS

Words and Music by
ROBIN LERNER, ANNIE ROBOFF
and BETH NIELSEN CHAPMAN

Moderately, with double-time feel ♩ = 64

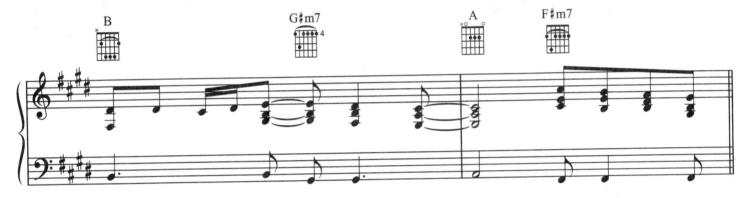

Verse:

1. I don't want an-oth-er heart-break. I don't need an-oth-er turn to cry,_____ no.
2. Cin-der-el-la said to Snow White, "How does love get so off course?"_____ Oh.

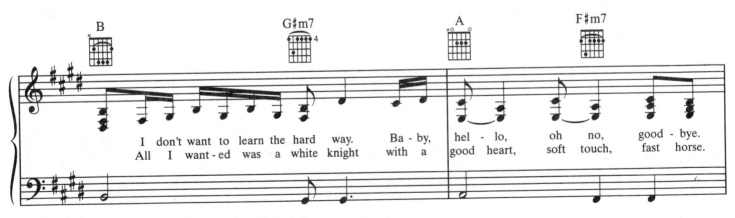

I don't want to learn the hard way. Ba-by,   hel-lo,   oh no,   good-bye.
All I want-ed was a white knight with a   good heart,   soft touch,   fast horse.

This Kiss - 4 - 1

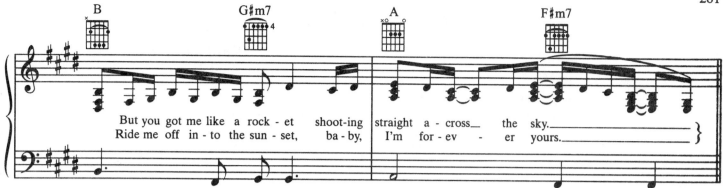

This Kiss - 4 - 2

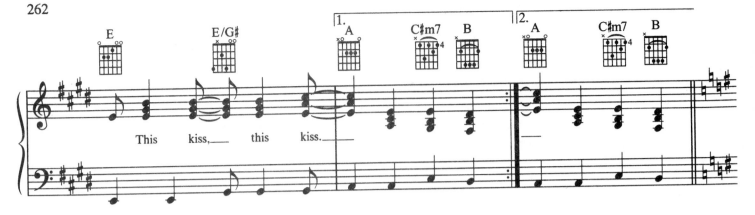

This kiss, this kiss.

Bridge:

You can kiss me in the moon-light, on the roof-top, un-der the sky, oh.

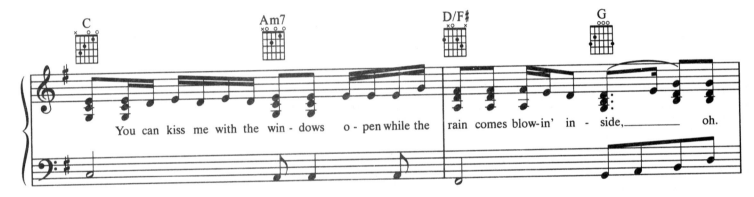

You can kiss me with the win-dows o-pen while the rain comes blow-in' in-side, oh.

Kiss me in sweet, slow mo-tion. Let's let ev-'ry-thing slide.

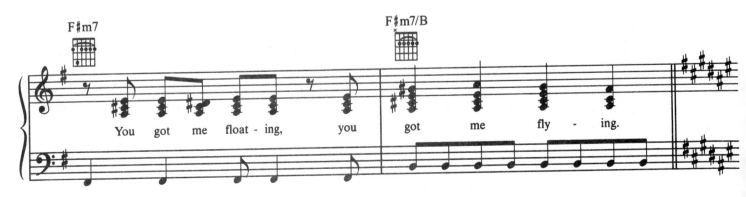

You got me float-ing, you got me fly-ing.

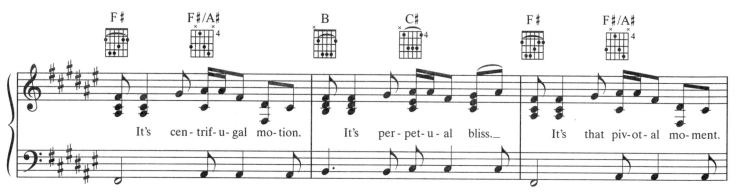

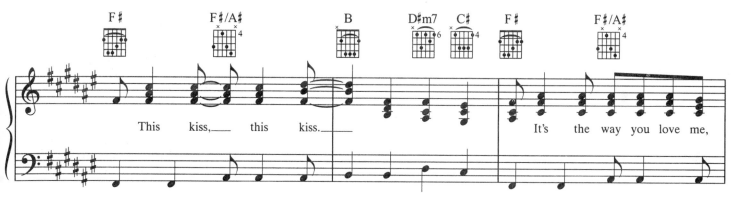

This Kiss - 4 - 4

YOU NEEDED ME

Words and Music by
RANDY GOODRUM

You Needed Me - 4 - 1

266

You Needed Me - 4 - 3

You Needed Me - 4 - 4

YOU WERE MEANT FOR ME

Words and Music by
JEWEL KILCHER and STEVE POLTZ

Moderate swing feel ♩ = 108

1. I hear the clock, it's six A. M.,
2.3. *See additional lyrics*

I feel so far from where I've been. I've got my eggs and my

You Were Meant for Me - 5 - 1

Verse 2:
I called my mama, she was out for a walk.
Consoled a cup of coffee, but it didn't wanna talk.
So I picked up a paper, it was more bad news,
More hearts being broken or people being used.
Put on my coat in the pouring rain.
I saw a movie, it just wasn't the same,
'Cause it was happy and I was sad,
And it made me miss you, oh, so bad.
(To Chorus:)

Verse 3:
I brush my teeth and put the cap back on,
I know you hate it when I leave the light on.
I pick a book up and then I turn the sheets down,
And then I take a breath and a good look around.
Put on my pj's and hop into bed.
I'm half alive but I feel mostly dead.
I try and tell myself it'll be all right,
I just shouldn't think anymore tonight.
(To Chorus:)